The Wee Ulster Phrase Book

DOREEN McBRIDE

ADARE PRESS
White Gables
Ballymoney Hill
Banbridge
Telephone: 028 - 4062 3782

Published by Adare Press
Typesetting by Adare Press and Banbridge Chronicle
Printed by Banbridge Chronicle

ISBN 1 899496 14 9

Contents

Introducshun

Ah've made it ma mission in life til help strangers unnerstan the most butiful language in the world, the language spoken here in Norn Iron. Them pur firreners don't speak as they shud. Tha morr tongue, of them wot lives across the sheugh, has become adulterated cos it's spread through tha world and is spoke by firreners everywhur. It's a cryin' shame, so tis. They've messed it all up.

Here in this small Province, whur not one sowl will budge an inch on any important issue, we have managed til preserve ar language. We have not allowed no-one nowhur til mess it up. We still speak perfect Shakespearean English an it is generally recognised that no-one spoke it better nor Willie Shakespeare. We have combined his language with tha most meaningful words from Gaelic and from Ulster Scots. We have tha culture others need and it's only rite til share it.

To that end I have already writ two books, 'Speakin' Norn Iron As She Shud Be Spoke'* an 'How Til Spake Ulster'. Tha research necessary for them books made me realise that them firrenerss are disadvantaged when they arrive here. We can hardly unnerstan a word wot thur tryin' til say. They talk funny. They, God help them, can hardly unnerstan us. Ah've decided til do something for them and have writ a book til help them larn til spake proper.

*Northern Ireland is known locally as 'Norn Iron'. The language spoken is 'Norn Iron' or 'Norn Ironspeak'.

Practise Makes Perfect

A practise exercise has been included at the end of each chapter. Students of Norn Iron speak are advised to attempt to translate this exercise into English and to read it aloud, preferably in front of a mirror, to perfect the pronunciation.

If several students are studying together it is recommended that they read the exercise aloud to each other and, as the exercises are written in the form of a monologue, see if they can either extend the monologue, or develop it into a dialogue.

When either extending the monologue, or developing a dialogue, try to incorporate some of the wonderful concepts which must be unique to Norn Iron speak, such as 'havin a fringe snokers ye fur wearin a hut', she wuz tarrible bad an' had a hysterical rectum'.

At The Hotel

Northern Ireland has excellent hotels, excellent food and friendly service. Obviously local people do not usually need to stay in local hotels. It is a small area. Locals usually prefer to escape the weather and spend their holidays in such places as Spain. There they have the opportunity to bask in the sunshine and share their culture.

It is possible to meet the occasional Norn Ironer in hotel lobbies enjoying a 'cheap weekend' advertised through the tourist board, or staying over after a wedding reception so that they do not have to worry about the drink-drive laws and can get, as they would say, blocked. Look out for and listen to these local stalwarts. They are wonderful.

It is also useful to have a few phrases to express yourself to hotel staff.

Suitable phrases for use on arrival at a hotel

Phrase	***Translation***
Have youse got a bed?	*Can you provide us with accommodation?*
Wot's tha dammitch?	*What is the price?*
Much yer lukin'?	*What is the price?*
Thon's desprit	*It is very expensive*
Thon's a shakin' price	*It is very expensive*
Thon's daylight rabbery	*It is very expensive*

Et's quare and posh	*This place appears to be very upmarket*
The hate ere's desprit	*It is too warm*
Ware's tha classit?	*Where is the rest room?*
Ah nee til pay a wee visit	*I need to visit the rest room*
Ah haf til visit the yard	*I need to visit the rest room*
Ware's tha rinal?	*Where is the gents' rest room?*
Cud ye gie us a shout in tha marnin'?	*We would like a morning wake up call*
When's brakfess?	*At what time is breakfast served?*
We cud do wif a male	*We could do with something to eat*

Suitable phrases to use as complaints in a hotel

Phrase	***Translation***
Tha room's piggin'	*The room is dirty*
Shire's busted	*The shower is not functioning properly*
Classit's all stuffed up	*The toilet is blocked*

Yer quare an mangy wif the sap	*You have not given us sufficient soap*
We ain't got no tiles	*We do not have any towels*
Cud we have more clothes on tha bed?	*Could we have more bed-clothes?*
Ware frizz	*We are cold*
Thon hate's desprit so tis	*The room is too warm*
Ah'm no feelin' so hot cos av tha hate	*The excess heat is making me feel ill*

Practise makes Perfect

Sez he til me sez, 'Cassie cum on, let's celerbrate ar thirtieth by spending a posh weekend in a posh 'otel. It'll be quare an romantic.'

Ye cud have knocked me down wif a feather. So ye cud.

Me? In a posh 'otel wif ar Alfie? An him mention the wurd 'romance'! Niver! Ah wundered wot he wuz up til. Romance? Onway he's quare an gud. A re-al gentilemon. He niver as much as lays a finner on me, so Ah luks at him an sez Ah til him, sez Ah, 'Dead on!'

An, yew know, we went! Jist the two of us.

When Ah got inside tha dur Ah jist stood an gauked, it wuz that posh. Ah wuz up til ma oxyters in carpet. An them chandeleears! Shinin, they wuz! Shinin! An tha hate! Desprit it wuz! Desprit.

An yew shud haf seen ar room! A great beg bed an a baff room an all. An tha baff room had enuff tiles in it til dry tha Salvation Army, so it had!

Eating Out

Eating out can be a wonderful experience in Norn Iron, especially in pubs and bars. Here it is possible to be lucky enough to hear the natives in full flight.

Where else would it be possible to hear such fascinating confessions as 'Ah had til stay in tha house cos ma corn wuz leppin', or 'My hur won't stay back aff ma face so Ah've got it cut intil a fringe. Havin' a fringe doesn't haf snooker ye fur wuring a hut,' or 'She wasn't at herself. 'She hurted her beg toe an was limpin' roun like a fella wif a wooden leg.'

USEFUL PHRASES

Requests for food

Phrase	*Translation*
Giv us a beg fry	*I would like a large fry*
Ah cud murder dip	*I am hungry and would like a fry*
Ah'd take sum sweeten	*I would like some wheaten bread*
Ye cannae bate vision cheps	*It is impossible to better fish and chips*
Giv us tha jeez bord	*I will have the cheese board*
Ah'm crazy bout griskens	*I really enjoy pork*
Wud ye pass tha oles?	*Would you pass the rolls?*

Giv us a wee bap	*Give me a soft roll*
Ah'd laike a wee pastie wif ma cheps	*I would like a pastie* with my chips*
Ah'll have peas wif ma cheps	*I would like peas with my chips*
Ah'd laike a lump av stak	*I will have steak*
Ah'll haf a bit av thaddick	*I will have the haddock*
I'd laike til dig intil a gud drap av parritch	*I would like some porridge*
Ah'd laike a chickon cyurry	*I would like a chicken curry*
Ah onny want a drap a tay	*I only require some tea*
A cap av calfee	*A cup of coffee*

** A local savoury delicacy of indeterminate origin and indeterminate content.*

Suitable complaints to use in a restaurant

Phrase	***Translation***
Thon dush's piggin	*That plate is dirty*
Thon tay's as wake as hawly whater in an Orange Lodge	*The tea is unbelievably weak*
Thon caffee's poisnus	*The coffee is poor*

Even the luk of yon wud make me turn	*That meal appears unappetising*
Thon wudnae lie aisy in ma stummick	*The meal would make me sick*
Thon gubs a dead loss. It's cowl	*The food is not up to standard. It is cold*
Ah wudnae giv thon til the dawg	*The food is inedible*

Suitable praise

Phrase	***Translation***
Thon wud putt hairs on yer chist	*That meal was excellent*
Thon puddin' wuz jist the jab	*The sweet was excellent*
Thon thaddick's dead on	*The haddock is excellent*
Thon stew's the quare stuff	*The stew was excellent*
Thon grub wuz wheeker	*The meal was excellent*
Thon grub wuz dead on	*The meal was excellent*
Thon's a rite beg feed	*That is a large helping*

Useful miscellaneous phrases

Phrase	***Translation***
Thon stable's dead on	*That table is satisfactory*
Y'ar	*The meal is being served*

Get bate intil yer mate	*Eat your meat*
Dig intil yer stew	*Eat your stew*
Ma jaws is workin' laike the grinder in McCartan's quarry on tha mate	*The meat is tough*
Ah'm grindin' awa 'ere an tha steak	*The steak is tough*
Thon waiter luks sif he'd putt his fat thumb in yer soup	*That waiter looks inefficient*
See yous waiters? Yer useless	*The service is extremely poor*
If yon wee waitress wud stap makin' sheep's eyes at yon fella we might git a bit av service	*That young waitress is not concentrating on her job because she is flirting with that gentleman*

Practise makes perfect

Ah wuz sittin in tha middle av me chips, in thon posh Chinese down than road, when ar wee Willie puts his hed in through tha door an lets a beg gulder aout av 'im. 'Ma! Ar team's won!' he gulders, as bawld as brass. Ah was morteefied, so Ah wuz. Evra hed turned. Ah cud feel maself goin' all red. Talk about yer hat flush! Et's nathin compared til wot Ah had in thon Chinese. Ar wee Willie's a re-al wee rip. He just done thon gulder out av sheer badness. He knowed Ah'd be emberarsed.

Still Ah wuz glad fur the chile. He's really in til futball. Takes it terrible serious, so he does. So Ah jest had a wee glass av wyne til celebrate and ar wee Willie had a beg coke.

Up The Pub

Local pubs provide more craic than any other institution, especially in rural areas. Locals come into swop yarns and there may be what I would think of as 'tasteful' music, that is music that is not too loud, is played by people who bring in their own instruments and is not pre-recorded. In a way it is like visiting a factory shop. It depends on what has come in on the day, or who has come down from the mountains.

My knowledge of pubic houses is limited, so the following is not a definitive list. The one in Mullabane, County Armagh frequently has music and storytelling. 'Wee Minnies' in Gilford, County Down may have traditional music and storytelling, while 'The Halfway' house in Annalong usually has a traditional accordion player at the weekends. He may be joined by other musicians, but that just depends on who is present.

Traditional musicians may sit in a circle, playing away like mad with a look of deep concentration. This means they are practising something together and do not want to be interrupted. If they are sitting in a semi-circle it may be taken as an invitation to produce your own instrument and join them.

It is very easy to get involved in interesting conversations in pubs. Alternatively I just like to sit and listen. The practice section at the end of this section is a transcript of a conversation I heard while having a pub lunch in 'The Homestead' at Ballyaughlis near Belfast. I have changed the names, but that is all.

The following phrases should help you to follow the conversation, or, alternatively, to join in.

Phrase	***Translation***
Yew cumin'?	*Are you coming with me (to the pub)?*
Aye! Ah'll hav a wee jar	*Yes. I would like a drink*
Ah wud nay say 'No' til a jar	*I would like a drink*
Ah'm stannin!	*I am buying this round of drinks*
Ah'll have a battle by tha neck	*I would like a bottle of beer*
Ah'll have a chin an tonic	*I would like a gin and tonic*
Ah'll have a fucken orange	*I would like vodka and orange*
Ah'll have a wee haf un	*I will have a short drink*
Ah'll have a wee haf un an a chaser	*I will have a half pint of Guinness and a whiskey*
Buy us a wee white wyne	*I would like a glass of white wine*
Ah'll see wot a pint ta pour wull do til me	*I will have a pint of porter*
Howl on. Ah'm rightly	*I really should not drink any more*
Sarry. M'af it. Ah'm drivin'	*I do not wish to consume alcohol because I am driving*

Luk at thon glass! S'empy!	*That glass needs a refill*
Luk at 'im. He's awa wif tha ban'	*Look at him. He's drunk*

He's stovin'	*He's drunk*
Thon fella's futless an legless forby	*He's drunk*
Thon fella cud nay bite his own thum	*He's drunk*
Ah'm plastered til the gills.	*I am drunk*
Ah'm as ful as a po	*I am drunk*
Do ye know? Ah'm nicely	*I am feeling slightly tipsy*
Lather in til it	*Drink up*
Cum on roun tha beck. Et's closed	*It is after closing time but we will be able to have a drink if we sneak in through the back door*

Ah'm fer hame ny afore Ah'm stovin	*I am going home now before I become inebriated*

Practise makes perfect

Conversation overheard in The Homestead, Ballyaughlis, near Belfast.

'Ah used til cum up the pub evra Friday night wif my mon, Shuey. Then he died. Ah wuz terrible lonely, Ah wuz. I jest stayed in tha house and moped. Then ma chum, Mildred, she sez til me, sez she,

'See you, Aggie, yer lettin' yersel go. So yew lost yer mon. Thon's a tradeadgee. But yer nat tha only wan. Other weemen have lost thur men and gone out an got thur get up an go. Yew'll jest haf to catch yersel on. Life goes on, so it does.'

An Ah thought about it. An Ah thought she wuz rite. An Ah started til cum out. An Ah started til ate again. An do yew know something? It done me a world av good. Of course Ah still miss ma Beg Shuey, so Ah do. But I jest get up in the mornin' an putt on a beg fry fur two. Two farls av soda bread, a couple av bets av tatie bread, a bet av bacon an a couple av eggs. An Ah giv Beg Shuey's breakfast til ar dog, Rover. An do ye know somethin'? He laves it. He ates it all up, egg an all.

Thur's only one thing wrong, so thur is. My next door naybor, Sadie, she seys til me, seys she, 'Do you see yon dog av yours? Et's got awful fat since yer Shuey died. Et's got an arse on it like ar Lizzie's.' And do ye know? She's rite.

Yew stannin? Ah'll hav a chin an tonic. Thenk ye kinly.'

On The Town

A night out in Norn Iron is pure entertaimemt, even if that sold by the management is poor. It provides the opportunity to view the locals at their best and evesdrop on fascinating snippets of conversation, such as 'Them uns is a pack av edjiots.', and 'I hate tha luks av them male dancers padded fronts. I sopose they mus ta got thurselves up laike thon to til let them weemen dancers clim up them laike thon. Dessgustin' so tis!'

At the Theatre

Phrase	***Translation***
She wuz singin laike she wuz getting her tubes tied	*The leading lady's top notes were shrill*
Them un's dead on	*It is an extremely successful performance*
Them uns is useless	*They not giving a good performance*
Them un's a dead loss	*It is a very poor production*
Thur makin' rite edjiots av thurselves	*The actors are making fools of themselves*
It wuz that boorn Ah cud harly keep m'eyes soapin'	*It was so boring I found difficulty in staying awake*
Ackt? Ma granny cud do batter	*My granny displays better acting talent*

Him an acktor? Don't make spit	*He does not display any me talent as an actor*
Thon wee thing can't haf act	*The leading lady is displaying a lot of talent*
Ah nearly laffed ma leg aff	*It was very amusing*
It wuz a quare geg	*It was very amusing*
Ah nearly split ma sides	*It was very amusing*
See thon male dancers - can't stan them	*I dislike male dancers*
Thon male dancers a pack av pouffs	*I do not believe the male dancers are heterosexual*
Luk at them pouffs poncin'	*I find the male dancers distasteful*
Luk at the cut av thon	*Look at the way that individual is dressed*
Do ye think thon style'll ever cum back?	*That mode of apparel is very outdated*
She's mutton dressed as lam	*The style in which she is dressed does not become her advanced years*

At the Cinema

Phrase	***Translation***
Ar yez cumin til tha pitchers?	*Would you like to go to the cinema?*

Wud ye laike til see a pitcher?	*Would you like to see a movie?*
Ah haven't been til tha flicks since tha Pope wuz a curate	*I have not been to a movie for some considerable time*
Do ye remembra Stanlie Whilee an his beg orgon	*Do you remember Stanley Wylie? (an organist who use to perform in the now defunct Ritz Cinema)*
Is this a sex certifekate?	*Is this an X-certificate?*
Ye'd near need a mortgage til git in til tha pitchers nydays	*Visiting the movies has become extremely expensive*
Saw rite fur tha weans?	*Is it suitable for children?*
She's got a gub laike a poun av bacon	*She has a very large mouth*
He's a quare hunk	*He is very good looking*
She's a wee dawl	*She is very good looking*
She's all ars an udder	*She is somewhat over endowed*
It wuz nathin but a lat av awl lave	*The love story was overdone*
It wuz tarrable slappy	*It was too sentimental*
Them speshal effects wuz wheeker	*The special effects were outstanding*

At a Disco

Phrase	***Translation***
Whur's the talen?	*Is there anyone I would consider attractive present?*
Thur's no talen here	*I do not find anyone here attractive*
Them weemen's a pack av dogs	*I do not like the women's appearance*
Luk at thon wee doll	*Look at that stunning girl*
Luk at thon beg hunk	*Look at that attractive man*
See him? He's got a hunchback!	*Do you observe that man? He drives a hatchback vehicle*
Luk at thon fella lepin laike a hen on a hot griddle	*Look at the energetic way that man is dancing*
Luk at tha goes av her	*Look at what she is doing*
Wotch him. When he's stovin he's violin	*Beware of him. He becomes violent when he has indulged in too much alcohol*
Luk at thon wee paneist. He's laverlee an the piano	*The pianist is excellent*
Luk at thon frock! Wot it's not hangin out it's pointing at	*That dress is immodest. It has a very low neck and a split skirt*

Ah'm nat dancing. Ah'm swaitin	*I am so hot I cannot dance*
Ah cud take ma dead end at him	*I find him very amusing*
Augh awa on	*You are teasing me*
Yer the quare geg	*I find you very amusing*
How about it?	*Would you like to become intimate?*
Get lost wee fella	*The answer is No!*

Practice Makes Perfect

Ah seen him at tha disco an he wuz leppin around laike a March hare.

Ah tuk one luk at him an sez Ah til masel, sez Ah,

'Thon's wan beg hunk. Ah cud do a thing or two fur a fella laike him. He's awful well putt on!'

Yew cud have knocked me down wif a feather when he cums up til me an sez,

'Ar yew dancing?' As bold as brass he wuz.

'No!' sez Ah, 'Ah'm fryin eggs tonite.'

Well! He starts wigglin all roun in fron av me. Yew shud have seen the goes av him. His legs whur fair whizzing roun.

'Cum on on in on tha flur,' sez he, 'quit yer fryin an feel tha bate. Be onselfish wif yer charms.'

Wosn't thon tha quare elegant way fur a fella til talk?

'Yer wish is granite!' sez Ah. An a tuk til tha flur wif him. Ah got til rack wif him all nite, then Ah got him til take me home. He's got a hunchback. An he's takin me out in his hunchback on Saturday. Isn't thon tha quare geg?

At The Wedding

Local weddings are fun. Enjoy!

Phrase	***Translation***
Would ye luk at tha per av them?	*Would you look at the pair of them?*
Thur jist dotin'	*They appear to be very much in love*
Thon bride luks as if she's in a tither	*The bride looks nervous*
Thon wee bride's laverlee	*The bride looks lovely*
She's gorjus	*She is looking very well*
The bride's morr's mutton dressed as lamb	*The bride's mother is dressed in a youthful fashion which is not suitable for her advanced years*
The bride's morr's got her titties in a tissy	*The bride's mother is obviously upset about something*
The groom's farr's awful corpulen!	*The groom's father is very fat*
Thon best mon was a quare turn	*The best man was very amusing*

Thon do musta cost a fortune	*The reception must have been very expensive*
Thon wee bride's maid's a rite wee terra	*The bride's maid is very amusing*
Ar Sammy, watch out for beg Hilda. She's flyin'. She'll be unner yew in a flash	*Sammy, beware of Hilda. She is drunk and will try to seduce you*
The bride's morr's one plite wee wumman	*The bride's mother is very well spoken*
The bride's farr luks laike he wuz in the peeritch	*The bride's father looks like a lord*
He's a quare fine fella	*He is a fine upstanding man*
She's lukee til get him	*The bride is fortunate in her choice of mate*

Practise Makes Perfect

Do ye see yon Painist? He's wan hunk! He's laverlee on tha paino. Ah cud get tha hats fur 'im. Ah'd lav til set up on tap av tha piano an cross ma legs an all, but Ah'm rightly. Ah cudn't get out av this chur an set an a bar stool. Ah'd fall aff, so Ah wud.

Thon wee bride's laverly ain't she? Mine yew, she's got her hans full. He's awful petted on his morr.

His morr's a rite awl cow. Verra possessive she is. Verra possessive. An talk about house proud! She wudn't let ye luk out av yer ees in 'er house. She's a terra. She hasn't been the same since she had her hysterical rectum. I reckon her homones is bothering her. She alwus seems til have her titties in a tissy, so she does. The farr, he's jest the apposite. Verra relaxed! Verra relaxed! If he whur much more relaxed he'd be dead.

Do yew see Beg Vera. Thon hut's terrible on her. Having a fringe fairly snookers ye fur wearing a hut. Wud ye jest luk at her! She's futless an' legless furby. She's the quare awul fool, Ah'm tellin' ye.

Still, it's been a laveree day. Musta cost a fortune! Beg Sadie seys it's such a laverlee day it wud almos giv her the notion til take tha plunge. She's batter hurry up Ah say. She's gettin past her sell by date. If she waits much longer she'll haf til wur a crinolin so she can shove her zimmer up it!

Mine ye, them young ones don't know thur livin' nydays. Startin thur lives together wif washin' machines an all. When ma Sammy (God rest his soul) and Ah started up we had nathin'. Nathin! Changed times.

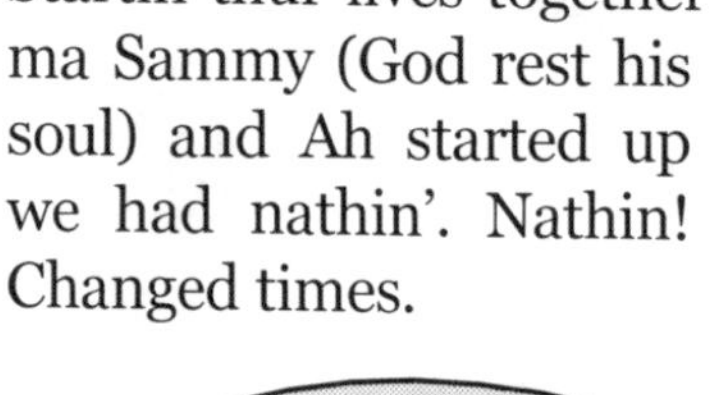

Sport

Football, rugby, hurling, ice hockey, they all have their enthusiastic vociferous supporters. A stiff upper lip is not an attribute at any local game. It is much better to let your hair down and join the fun. Language is not really needed. Any expressive yell will do, especially if it is accompanied, where appropriate, by jumping up and down with joy, or covering the eyes in sorrow. However, for advanced students of the language the following phrases are suitable for any game that is played in a stadium.

Suitable phrases to shout encouragement

Phrase	***Translation***
Go on ye boys!	*Well done!*
Get stuck in!	*Try harder!*
Shove it up em!	*That was a good pass/shot/goal/etc.,*
Stickin' out!	*Very well done!*
Thon wan's tynamite!	*They are extremely talented!*

Suitable phrases to express disappointment/disapproval

Phrase	*Translation*
Ar wans can't play fur champ	*Our team is off form*
Ref's an edjiot!	*The referee is very stupid!*
Ref's lost 'is bap!	*The referee is crazy!*
Ref's haf cut!	*The referee is drunk!*
Ar wan's'll get stuffed!	*Our team is going to loose the match*
Shoot the ref!	*The referee should be shot!*
Thon wan's is futless!	*That team is playing badly!*
Ah cud do better masel wif no arms!	*I could play better myself even if I was without arms!*
Them bex is useless!	*The backs are useless!*
On yer bike!	*You should go home!*

Practise Makes Perfect

Ah dinnae laike sport. Mine yew, my wee Willie's crazy about it. Ye cannae live wif him when his team looses. Takes it til heart, so he does. Gits all upset. Ah wunner that he bathers. Ah see no sense in getting my titties in a tizzy just cos some edjiot loss his ball in Winser Pork. Thurs naw point in it. An as fur them futball hulligans. They shud put them awa so they shud. Bring back the birch, Ah say. It wud larn them a bit av sense. Nydays thurs no detergent. Them young wans jist do as they laike. An if they git caught, so wot! Up affore tha judge an if they git time thur sent til a halliday camp, wif T.V.s an all. An who's payin fur it tall? Us! The pur tax payer.

Its nat fur, so it's nat. An if yew an I git caught speeding, wot happens? Whur had.We haf til pay up. Thur's no justice, so thur's nat.

Mine yew - Ah felt tarrible sarry fur ar wee Willy on Saturdey. When Ah came home from seein ma morr thur he wuz, settin in the kitchen drinkin beer. Ah thought he was celebratin. He wussnae. He wuz drowin his sarraws. An then he went in til tha closit an thoed rings roun him, rings roun him. Ah felt sore sarry fur the wee sawl, so Ah did! He takes it tarrable searus.

In Case Of Illness

Some very interesting illness exist in Norn Ironspeak, such things as 'information of the kidneys', 'sectarian operations' and a 'wee whinge in tha knee'.

At the Chemist

Phrase	*Translation*
Shemist	*Chemist*
M'eers botherin' me	*My ears are sore*
Cud ye give us cattan wool for m'eers	*I need some cotton wool for my ears*
Ah can't hear m'eers	*I have gone deaf*
Ma hed's splittin	*I have a sore head*
Ah'got information av tha thum	*My thumb is inflamed*
Ah'm nat at masel. Ah've bin bealin'	*I do not feel well. I keep vomiting*
Ah won't be at masel til Ah get ma legs back	*I will not feel well until my legs are better*
Me feet ar laike baps	*My feet are swollen*
Cud ye giv us something fur ma caff?	*Could I have something for my cough?*
Ah want til get rid av ma chist	*I want something to cure my sore chest*
Cud ye giv us some thin til stick on ma blister?	*Have you any plasters?*

At the Doctor's

Phrase	*Translation*
M' ulster's bust	*I fear that my ulcer has burst*
Ah whant ta git rid av m'awl stummick	*I have a bad pain in my upper abdomen*
Nathin' will lie in ma stommick	*I keep vomiting*
Ah've gat this thote fur near a week	*My throat has been troubling me for approximately a week*
Nixt Tuesay Ah'll av been bad fur a fortnite	*On Tuesday I will have been ill for two weeks*
Cud ye banditch m'ankle?	*Would you strap my ankle*
Ah've vines	*I believe I am suffering from varicose veins*
Ah've got veronica's vines	*I believe I am suffering from varicose veins*
M'arm'spoke	*I have broken my arm*
Cud Ah git m'eers singed?	*I believe I need wax removed from my ears*
I fell intil a sheugh an got a skalf in ma thum	*I fell into a ditch and got a thorn stuck into my thumb*
Cud ye giv us somethin' til bring tha information in ma thum til a hed?	*I have a suppurating thumb*

Ah spittin'. Ah'm preggan agin	*I am upset because I am pregnant again.*
Ma hed's goin' roun an roun. Ah had til walk on ma dauter's arm til git here	*I have such bad vertigo I needed assistance from my daughter to enable me to reach here*
M'arts tarrable bad	*I am worried about the pain in my chest*
Ah want ma tubes tied	*I would like to be sterilised*
Ma shaulder's half killin' me	*I have a sore shoulder*
Ah haven't drawn breath fer a fortnight	*I have been breathless for two weeks*

At the Chiropodist's

Phrase	***Translation***
Chirapaddist	*Chiropodist*
Ma fet's killin' me	*My feet are sore*
Ma fet's takin' tha legs av me	*My feet are sore*

Ma fet's laike baps	*My feet are swollen*
Ma corns is leppin	*My corns are troubling me*
Ah've got an ingroan toe	*I have an in growing toenail*
Ma beg toe's desperate	*My big toe is very sore*
Them bunyons is tarrable	*My bunions are extremely sore*
Ma chews hav made a rite haun av ma feet	*My shoes are hurting my feet*
Ah've near walked the balls av ma legs roun the front	*I have travelled a long distance on foot*
Ah futted it ivvery fut av tha way here	*I arrived here on foot*
Ah won't be at maself til Ah get ma legs back	*The walk tired me*

Practise makes perfect

Ah decided til go til the city til get get ma tubes tied. After all Ah had sex! Sex's enuff. They wud turn yer hed, so they wud.

Ah went on the bus 'cos Ah had walked the legs aff maself on Sunday in the cemerrtary. It was ma morr's anniversary so Ah went til putt flours on her grave. It's a tarrable long walk from the gates til ma morr's grave. Tha balls av ma legs wuz near roun the front, so they wur.

Well anyway, thon wee nurse sed til me, sed she, 'Hev a specimen when yew come beck.' She wuz awful plite so she wuz. Ah cud fin nathin but a wee whiskey battle til putt my specimen in, so Ah cudn't. An do yew know wot? Somebudy stole it on tha bus! Ye cudn't watch them nowadays, cud ye?

Ah've lost all my modesty since ah started goin' til thon 'ospital. It's desperate wot them dacters an nurses do til ye, so 'tis! Desperate!

Ah wuz on ma back when thon beg dacter sez til me, sez he.

'So ye've had sex?'

'Yes, dacter,' sez Ah, 'Sex. Ah want ma tubes tied.'

'Sex childer is enough fur anywan,' sez he, 'Ah certainly have no objection til orchestrating ye.'

'Yew'd haf thought Ah wuz the cyat, so ye wud.'

'An,' sez he, 'Wot age is yer youngest.'

'Sex,' sez Ah, as bold as brass.

'An wot kind av contraception are ye using?' sez he.

'Nathin!' sez Ah.

'Nathin'?' sez he. 'Nathin'? Do ye really think ye need til be orchestrated? Ah wud doubt it as it's been so long since tha birth av yer youngest chile. Wot makes ye think ye need til be orchestrated.'

'Ah jest tol him, so ah did. Wot wif this early release an all, ma mon's getting' out av prison an ah want til be ready fur him, so Ah do.'

At A Funeral

Most Irish people have a tendency to joke, laugh, have fun at most unsuitable occasions. Funerals are no exception. A good laugh makes pain more bearable. The death of a child, or a sudden death are obviously heart breaking, otherwise death is accepted as a part of life and is treated philosophically and while the funeral service itself will be treated solemnly, the rest of the proceedings will probably be a pleasant social occasion.

Remnants of the age-old tradition of the wake still survive, especially in rural areas. It is still possible to see a coffin being carried, by four men, towards a graveyard with mourners following walking in a solemn procession behind and a line of cars driving at walking speed behind them.

Traditionally, it was only the men who travelled with the body to the cemetery while the women stayed in the deceased's house and prepared a meal for the men to eat when they returned. This tradition has changed so that mourners walking behind a coffin now often are graced by the presence of women. The tradition of the meal remains unchanged, but wake games, that is games played for the days in which the corpse remained in his/her home before the funeral service and burial took place, have died out.

The following phrases could puzzle a stranger. I, for the sake of clarity, have made them applicable to men. They are equally applicable to women. Expect the type of contradictary sayings common in Ireland such as 'Is this whur tha ded mon lives?' Strangers may also be perturbed by phrases such as 'She's quare and cut up.' This simply means she was very upset. There has not been a knife attack!

It is deemed polite to show respect by eating a hearty meal at the funeral feast.

Phrase	*Translation*
He's waitin' on	*He is expected to die in the next few hours*
He died av a Friday	*He died on Friday*
Ah'm sarry about yer trabble	*I am sorry you have been bereaved*
It wuz terrible sudden	*Death came suddenly*
It must haf bin a terrible shack	*It must have been a terrible shock*
Is this whur tha ded mon lives?	*Is this where the dead man lives?*
He didn't appear til die av anything serious	*He did not have a long illness*
She's quare an cut up	*She is very upset*
She's keepin up	*She is showing courage in the face of adversity*
Wud ye laike til view tha bady?	*Would you like to see the corpse?*
He's laverly lukin' in his caffin	*The corpse looks well*
He's lukin' quare an well	*The corpse looks well*
Thon unnertaker dun tha quare jab	*The undertaker did a good job*
He's had a hard time	*He suffered a lot*
He's quare an comfortable lukin'	*He looks comfortable*

He's 'appy at long last	*He is in a better world now.*
It's lucky fur him	*He has escaped the troubles of this world*
He's in a battar place	*He is in Heaven*
His broor's a dead loss	*I do not like his brother*
The corpse's broor wants til know, wot yer havin'?	*The brother of the deceased wants to know if you would like to partake of an alcoholic beverage*
Wud ye fancy a lift?	*Would you like to take a turn at carrying the coffin?*
The flurs is laverly	*The wreaths are beautiful*
Them flurs is tarrable deer	*Funeral wreaths are extremely expensive*
Them wee bun's is laverly	*The cakes are delicious*
Thon's tha quare bit av ham	*The cooked ham is delicious*
Ye done him proud	*It was a successful day*
It's a pity he missed it. He'd haf taken his ded end at it	It is a pity he could not attend his funeral. He would have enjoyed it

Practise makes perfect

This is a true story. It was told to me by a friend who immigrated to New Zealand. Thank you Shirley.

Ar Francie an her mon whur tarrable close, tarrable close. Ah thought it wud be tha end av her when he snuffed it. He caught a kiddenee disease. Tarrable sudden it wuz, tarrable sudden. An he wuz only farty.

Ar Francy wuz beside herself. Distracted she wuz, distracted. But she had him cemented. Thon Cementorium dun a loverly service so they dun and ar Francie surprised us all, so she did. She sed, 'Life has til go on. I'll haf til keep up for tha sake av Wee Jem.' Wee Jem was a wee only chile, ye know, an they doted on him, doted.

Onyway, Ar Fancie had her mon's ashes putt in a plastic beg in a loverly wee china ginger char, with a tap on it an all. She kapt tha char on tha mantelpiece an she used til talk to it. Sure it gave her comfort and she wuz doin no one no harm no how. She used til tell the char all her worries an how her Wee Jem wuz doin at school an all. Ah think she tald her mon more after he wuz ded than she did before. Well, he culdn't answer back, cud he? When Wee Jem got a place at the Unerversity she wuz over tha moon, over tha moon. The minute he gat his affer she rushed intil the parlour an tald the char all about it.

Eventually she saves up an decides to go an see her saster in New Zealan, so she did. Wee Jem wuz lef in charge av tha house, so he wuz. Well he wuz over 18 an sansable.

Wee Jem had a great time when she wuz awa, so he did. Then a couple av days afore she wuz due back he decided til haf a party. He invited all his wee frens an it wuz a great party.

After they had all gone home Wee Jem went til tidy up. Distracted he wuz! Distracted! Someone had knocked the china char over on the mantelpiece an tha lid had cum aff it, an all, an it wuz empy. Empy! Wee Jem thought, so he did, that someone had tidied up his farr's ashes. He thought his morr wud go mad if she foun his farr missin. He din't know what til do! Then he had a brain wave. He gat anorr plastic beg an collected all tha ash he cud from about tha place, cigarette ash, ash fram tha barbeeque, ash from tha fire place an all, an he dun it up jist like his farr's ashes and putt it intil the char.

When ar Francie came home she shot straight intil tha parlour and near went bananas.

'Who's thon stranger in yer farr's char?' she asked.

She'd taken tha ashes til New Zealan! Sed she wuldn't have gone without them. She wuz lucky them customs didn't mistake them fur cannabis or somethin'!

Going Shopping

Making purchases is locally known as 'goin shappin'. Local men, whose language is, I have to say with regret, both politically incorrect and sexist, say 'Weemen ar only good fur shappin an yappin!'

Phrase	***Translation***
Cumin shappin?	*Would you like to come shopping with me?*
Wud ye laike til go in ear?	*Would you like to enter this shop?*
Sa poun	*The price is £1*
Tree* poun	*The price is three pounds*
Poun a shuggar	*One pound of sugar*
Haf poun a tay	*Half a pound of tea*
Sum Ferry Lickwood	*I require some 'Fairy Liquid'*
Poun a sassitches	*A pound of sausages*
Giv us a bit av smoke addict	*I want some smoked haddock*

*There are many dialects within Norn Iron Speak so many words have different ways of being pronounced. Three is one of those words. Sometimes, depending on the locality and the origin of the speaker, it is prounced 'tree' other times 'thee'.

A bax a chawklats	*A box of chocolates*
A packet a pees	*A packet of dried peas*
A cabbitch	*A cabbage*
Ah luv til drink tha cabbitch whater	*I enjoy drinking the water in which the cabbage has been boiled*
A bunch a scallions	*Some spring onions*
Sex oranchez	*Six oranges*
Thee civil oranchez	*Three Seville oranges*
Poun a goosegabs	*A pound of gooseberries*
A'll hav a couple a carts	*A couple of carrots*
A char a aliffs	*A jar of olives*
A char a calfee	*A jar of coffee*
Thurs a dinge in this tin	*This tin is dented*
Ah cud do wif a perr a mutton dummies	*I could do with a new pair of training shoes*
The chile needs a perr a gutties	*The child needs a new pair of canvas shoes with rubber soles*
Ar Sadie's lukin a perr a boots	*My relative, Sadie, needs a new pair of boots*
Thons a cracker purr av jeans	*That is a very nice pair of jeans*

Ah need a perr a chews fur warin	*I need a pair of practical shoes to wear every day*
Ah'd laike a perr a chews, but nat fur warin	*I would like a pair of shoes for special occasions*
The price av a perr a tights 'scriminal	*Women's tights are outrageously expensive*
Wud ye evar putt a stamp on this?	*Please put a stamp on this*
Do Ah need a leff han stamp?	*Do I need an air mail stamp?*
Tha stamp fell on me	*I have dropped the stamp*
Postitche is tarrable deer	*Postage is very expensive*
Shappin's sickenin	*I do not like shopping*

Practise Makes Perfect

Ah near walked tha legs av masel on Saturday lukin a new suit fur church, nat fur warin. My Kevin came wif me an he's a ded loss at shappin. He's tarrable impaishen. Ah wen in til 'McMurray's' sale. They've sum quare guid stuff in thur sale an the place wuz crowded.

Ah laike 'McMurray's'. It luks a bit auld fashioned, an it's proper desperate getting upthem sturs, wot wif ma bad leg an all, but thur nice people an as Ah sey, thur stuff's guid. They've proper changin rooms wif a pit av privacy an all. Ah laike that. Ah hate strippin down til ma knickers wif onlookers. Ah feel so emberaresed so Ah do!

Ah foun a nice wee suit an wen intil a changing room til try it on.

My Kevin stud around tha shap lukin stupid, laike men do in shaps. He became impaishen. He thought Ah wuz takin a tarrable long time tryin on a suit. He wen til tha changing room an flung beck tha curtain.

'Will ye putt a move on!' seys he.

An he near drapped ded! Thur wuz a strange womon stanin in her bra an pants. He wuz that lucky she didn't scream!

Ah had gone til take ma suit til the till!

Travel

Norn Iron natives, as a rule, love strangers. As travellers they are compulsive talkers and are eager to engage in conversation.

There are two types of native travellers from Norn Iron, those who love it and greet the whole experience with enthusiasm and those who are so terrified they are generally sick. Thankfully the latter type is relatively rare, but beware of anyone who says anything like, 'Ah'm about til boke' Or 'Ah want til tho aff', especially if it is said by an elderly overweight woman.!

There is no need to be alarmed if someone starts to talk to you. Most people will just be interested in you as a person, where you are from, where you are going and what you think of Ireland. If you do not want to engage in conversation simply to express a derogatory sentiment about Ireland! Locally there is no quicker way to be end a conversation!

Phrases used to start up a conversation with a stranger.

Phrase	***Translation***
Whur err yer fur?	*Where are you going?*
Whurr err yer fram?	*Where are you from?*
It's the quare wather we'er havin	*We have been having good weather*
It's quare an cauld	*The weather has turned cold*

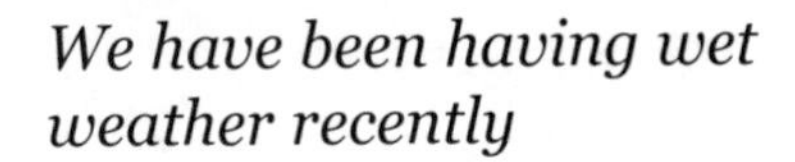

It's bin bucketin fur days	*We have been having wet weather recently*
Houlin up?	*Are you all right?*
How' ye mannijin?	*Can you manage?*
Hows about ye?	*Hello!*
Form awe rite?	*Are you in good form?*
Kaipin fit?	*Are you feeling fit?*

By Air

Phrase	***Translation***
Ah laike til go fline	*I like flying*
Ah'm afeared av fline	*I am frightened of flying*
Ah cannae fly unless Ah'm well oiled	*I cannot fly unless I have had a lot of alcohol*
Can Ah truss tha pilate?	*Do you think we have an experienced pilot?*

Ah think thon pilate's a larner driver	*I do not think the pilot is qualified*
S'late agen	*The plane is delayed again*
Fline makes me want til tho up	*Flying makes me feel sick*
Hope it doesn't start me vamitin	*I hope the experience of flying does not make me vomit*
Ah hate them pumps	*I hate turbulence*
'spumpy!	*It is turbulent*
Wen do we lite?	*When do we arrive?*
Ah'm goin til Landan	*I am travelling to London*
Ah'm goin' til Noo Yorak	*I am travelling to New York*

By Sea

Phrase	***Translation***
Whur do ye ketch tha boat fur Lile av Mon?	*Where do you get the ship for the Isle of Man?*
Goin til Lirpool?	*Are you travelling to Liverpool?*
Ah've a tarrable wake stummack	*My stomach is easily upset*
Ah'm goin til tho aff	*I am going to be sick*
Thon scringin does ma hed in	*The engine noise upsets me*

Membra 'The Princess Victoria'?	*Do you remember 'The Princess Victoria'? (A ferry that sank in The Irish Sea while travelling from Scotland to The North of Ireland in the early 1950's.)*
Ah shud av knowed batter	*I should known not to come*

By Car

Phrase	*Translation*
Wud ye laike a wee taste av petral?	*Do you need petrol?*
Thon awl wreck's niver out av tha garritch	*This car is giving me a lot of trouble*
Shove a wee pinta th'oil intil her	*I need a pint of oil*
My cyarr gulps th'oil at a rate av knots	*My car uses a lot of oil*
Take a wee geek at th'oil	*Assess if the car needs oil*

Wash ma windys, wud ye?	*Wash my windscreen*
Giv us a drap av win	*The car's tyres need air*
Ah've gat a flat	*I have a flat tyre*
Ah've gat a pumpture	*I have a puncture*
Much d'Ah haf til pay?	*How much do I owe you?*
Don't stap an a double yella	*Do not stop on double yellow lines*
Watch yer speed are the pollice will av ye up	*Watch your speed or the police will punish you*
Thon poliss do nathin til do bat catch speeders!	*The police do nothing but but catch people who are speeding*
Ah hate a farren cyar	*I hate foreign cars*
Ah'm buggered in Belfas trafick	*I find traffic in Belfast difficult to negotiate*
If Ah park here do Ah risk bein had up?	*Is it legal to park here?*
Ah drove all roun	*I travelled a great distance by car*

Practise Makes Perfect

Ah've never been out av Norn Iron, only onect, an Ah ain't niver goin agin, nohow.

Ma fren, Jinty, sed til me, sed she,

'How's about goin on a day trip til Lisle av Mon?'

Ah jist knowed Ah sud say 'No!', but ar Jinty's tarrable perswavif, so Ah went.

Niver again!

The minit Ah got on thon boat my stomack started heavin, an we hadn't even went out av tha harbour yit.

Ar Jinty seys til me,

'Cum up on tha deck an yew'll be purfectly alrite.'

'Purfectly alrite? Ah boked rings roun me, Ah did. Ah thought my end wuz in sight. Ah wuz niver so glad til see dry lan. An then my stomack turned at the thought av havin til git back. Ah spent tha day in the Treminal wif ma hans over ma eeys, cryin cos Ah had til git back. Ah niver saw nathin. Ah must have luked as if Ah'd bin pulled thew a hedge backwards. People kept lukin at me an Ah wuz all cut, as Ah wuz.

My dauter is something different, min yew. She an her mon took thur cyar over til France on a beg boat. They slep on it an all an when they got aff they drove all roun. She seys the closits in France are something shakin, so she does. She says tha ladies an gants all go in tilgether an that tha gants stan at them rinals an do what they have til do an that you can stan an wotch them. Shakin! Ah'm playin safe. Ah'm stayin in Norn Iron.

See Me? So Ah Did and So'Tis

A language, in addition to vocabulary, possesses a structure and a rhythm. Norn Iron speak owes a lot to its unique rhythm, which adds colour and tone and sheer poetry to everyday language.

It is no wonder that poets of the calibre of Seamus Heaney were born and raised in the Province. He cannot but have been influenced by the beautiful language which surrounded him during his formative years.

'See me?' 'So Ah did' and 'So'tis' are examples of phrases which, when added to sentence structure, add colour and rhythm to local speech.

Expressing preferences - The use of 'See me?'

'See me?' is a device locals use to add an air of colourful inquiry to the subject of their conversations.

'See me? See bacon? Can't stan it!' simply means 'I do not like bacon.'

Repeat the above phrase aloud several times stressing the first word in every sentence, until you feel the rhythm.

'See me? See bacon? Can't stan it!'

It is very easy to add another person to the sentiment.

Phrase	***Translation***
'See me? See ma man? See cheese? Can't stan it!'	*My husband/partner and I do not like cheese!*
'See me? See ma Morr? See cheese? Can't stan it!'	*My mother and I do not like cheese!*

The use of 'See me' to express a liking

'See me?' may also be used to express a liking.

Phrase	*Translation*
'See me? See bacon? 'S'wheeker!'	*I really like bacon!*

'See me?' used to express a sense of well being

Phrase	*Translation*
'See me? Ah'm dead on!'	*I am very well*
'See me? Ah cud sit up an ate an egg'	*I am feeling very well*
'See me? Ah'm spot on target!'	*I am progressing well*

'See me?' used to express a feeling of being off-form

Phrase	*Translation*
'See me? Ah'm nat at mesel'	*I do not feel well*
'See me? Don't know wots wong wif me.'	*I feel off form*
'See me? Ah feel laike tha wreck av tha Hesperous'	*I do not feel I am looking my best*
'See me? Ah feel laike Ah've bin pulled thu a hedge backwards'	*I fear I look extremely untidy*

'See her?' : 'See him?

'See her?' and 'See him?' are variants on 'See me?' They may be used as above and may also be used to express likes and dislikes for individuals.

Phrase	*Translation*
'See him? He's dead on!'	*He is a very fine person*
'See her? She's smashin!'	*She is a great person*
'See her? Thinks she's no goat's toe!'	*She has an inflated opinion of herself*
'See her? See's a heart av corn'	*She is always ready to give a helping hand*
'See him? His awn Morr cudn't laike him!'	*No one could possible like him*
'See him?' Ah cudn't laike him if Ah'd knitted him masel!'	*I could not like him under any circumstances*

So Ah Did!

'So Ah did' is used to emphasise a point. Listen to conversations and you will find speakers who give extra rhythm to their speech by repeating 'So Ah did!' at frequent intervals.

Phrase	*Translation*
'Ah bought a new pur av chews on Friday, so Ah did!'	*I bought a new pair of shoes on Friday*

h giv her a gud reddin' out, Ah did!'	*I scolded her severely.*
h tawl him til catch himself ı, So Ah did!'	*I suggested that he learn to be more sensible*
h did done it yesterday, ı Ad did!'	*I accomplished that yesterday in spite of your sceptism*

ariations on So Ah Did!

io Ah did' may be modified into 'So he did', 'So she did' and io y'are!'

hrase	*Translation*
He tol her til shut her ackin' ake, so he did!'	*He requested that she be silent*
She tol him to P.O., so she did!'	*She suggested that he go away*
Yer a gran lass, so y'ar'	*You are a great girl*

So 'tis!

'So 'tis is another phrase added on to the end of a sentence to add poetic rhythm to Norn Iron language.

Phrase	*Translation*
'It's the quare day, so 'tis!'	*It is a very fine day*
'It's cumin down stair rods, so 'tis!'	*It is raining heavily*

Other Books By Doreen McBride...

GREAT VERSE TO STAND UP AND TELL THEM
Edited by Doreen McBride

'Great Verse To Stand Up And Tell Them' captures the rich tapestry of life in North Ireland in comic verse. Every 'poem' has a situation story to tell and many are true to l But that's only to be expected from a writing team including Maud Steele, Billy Ritc Seamus Lavery, Bill Nesbitt and Crawford Howard. Doreen McBride has edited this bo She has done an excellent job producing a book that provides an excellent read with ver suitable for reciting as 'party' pieces or performing at local festivals. **Price £4.99**
'A tool of rare quality for those wishing to perform a party piece or enter a local festiv
'BELFAST TELEGRAPH'

A BIT OF CRAIC FROM BELFAST
by Doreen McBride

Illustrated by cartoon drawings and photographs of Belfast landmarks, th entertaining book takes us through the rich language usage of Belfast in a series of loc anecdotes and stories, accompanied by a working vocabulary. The book is also enliven by comic verse of local writers Crawford Howard, Raymond Calvert and Bill Nesb while Seamus Lavery's *'My Wee House'* adds a poignant reminder of the effects of inn city development. This book is a must for locals rejoicing in their heritage and for visito who wish to capture Belfast's character. **Price £4.50**
'An entertaining book.' NEWS LETTER
'A gem of a book.' IRISH NEWS

HOW TIL SPAKE ULSTER
by Doreen McBride

In this hilarious beginners' guide to speaking the language spoken in Northern Irelan Doreen McBride takes us by means of annotated cartoon and essential vocabulary t understanding some of the grammatical construction so essential to speaking the nativ tongue of her beloved Province. **Price £4.99**
'Doreen McBride did not come up the Lagan in a bubble.' Irish News

SPEAKIN' NORN IRON AS SHE SHUD BE SPOKE
by Doreen McBride

This local bestseller aims to help foreigners understand and appreciate the language spoken in Northern Ireland, which is affectionately referred to as 'Norn Iron' by local residents. As Doreen McBride explains, 'People coming from outside Norn Iron spake with a strange accent. It's very difficult to unnerstan them. After listenin' to people from all over, an' hardly understanin' wot thar tryin' til say, Ah've decided to do something about it an' produce a dictsunary til help foreigners spake proper.' This she has done and the result is hilarious. **Price £4.99**
'Essential reading' Gerry Kelly on 'Kelly' U.T.V.